FRONT
OSCAR
THE CAT THAT BEAT THE BURGLARS

Oscar

written by ANNE McKIE

illustrated by KEN McKIE

Two stories about Oscar, the cat who lived in a Joke Shop, written using a controlled vocabulary. All the books in the Storyboard series are at Level 5 + in the Key Words Reading Scheme and details are given at the back of the book. These books are also ideal for use as supplementary readers with any other reading scheme.

First edition

© LADYBIRD BOOKS LTD MCMLXXXIII

62340

Oscar
beats the burglars

Ladybird Books Loughborough

The shop next door to the Joke Shop
was a Jeweller's Shop.

Oscar liked to look at all the jewels in the window.

Sometimes he went into the shop
to see the Jeweller.

6

At night when it was dark,
the shops were closed.

Then Oscar played with the mice.
They lived in the Joke Shop too.

7

One night it was very dark.
The wind blew and lightning flashed.

The mice wanted to play at **ghosts**!

They made a ghost noise.
They made ghost shapes.

They tried to frighten Oscar.

But Oscar was not frightened.
He was fast asleep.

Then the mice got ready for bed
and one by one they went to sleep.

The mice woke up
and then Oscar woke up.

"What's that noise?" they said.
TAP, TAP, TAP, it went.

Oscar and the mice listened.
"The noise is in the Jeweller's Shop."

"Let's go into the shop and see what
it is," they said.

13

Two men, with masks on, were
putting the jewels into a bag.

"They are burglars," said Oscar.
"What shall we do?"

The mice were frightened.

They ran to a clock to hide.
"Come out," said Oscar.

He had an idea.
"Go back to the Joke Shop and bring
lots of jokes and tricks," he said.

The mice soon came back with
lots of jokes and tricks.

Oscar and the mice went behind the
burglars and made noises.

A mouse made a noise like a ghost.
"What's that?" said one burglar.

Oscar made a noise like a ghost.
"What's that?" said the other
burglar.

19

Then Oscar and the mice played with
all the jokes and tricks.

The burglars were very frightened.

"It's **ghosts**!" cried the burglars.

They ran to the door as fast as they could.

2

"Stop them!" said Oscar,
and the mice were ready to trip up
the two men.

The burglars tripped and the mice
played lots of tricks on them.

They could not get away.
Soon the burglars were tied up.

"Ring the alarm bell!" cried Oscar.

The Police heard the bell and came to take the burglars away.

Next day the Jeweller said, ''You were very brave. I shall give you all a medal.''

Oscar
plays the game

On Saturdays lots of people go by
the Joke Shop.
They are going to the football match.

30

They all wave to Oscar.
He is in the window of the shop.

"I wish I could go to a football
match," said Oscar, one Saturday.

The mice laughed at him.
"Cats don't go to football matches."

This made Oscar very cross.

The mice gave Oscar some milk.

Then they had a good idea to make Oscar happy.

Next door to the Joke Shop was a Sports Shop. "We will go and play in there," they said.

That night they went into the
Sports Shop.

This shop was full of games
and toys.

"Let's have some fun," said the
mice, and they did.

The mice played tennis.

Then they played with a roller skate.

Next they tried boxing and golf.

Soon Oscar was happy again.
He played with lots of games.

He played snooker.

Then the mice said, "Come and see what we've found."

4

It was a football game.
Now Oscar could play football.

Oscar tried to play . . .
but he was *too big!*

Oscar was
unhappy again.

"Look at this!" said a mouse.
It was a whistle.

44

So now Oscar could be the referee.

Oscar blew his whistle.

He blew his whistle lots of times.
He got cross with the mice.

They played football all night.
Then they went to sleep, in the
Sports Shop.

Next day a man came into the shop.

He was a footballer.
He found Oscar and the mice.

48

He laughed. ''Would you like to come
to a *real* football match?'' he said.

Oscar said, ''Yes.''
He was very happy.

Now Oscar and the mice go to a
football match *every* Saturday.

Notes to parents and teachers

This series of books is designed for children who have begun to read and who need, and will enjoy, wider reading at a supplementary level.

The stories are based on Key Words up to *Level 5c* of the Ladybird Key Words Reading Scheme.

Extra words and words beyond that level are listed below.

Words which the child will meet at *Level 6* are listed separately, in case the parent or teacher wishes to give extra attention to these words and use this series as a bridge between reading levels.

Although based on Key Words, these books are ideal as supplementary reading material for use with any other reading scheme. The high picture content gives visual clues to words which may be unfamiliar and the consistent repetition of new words will give confidence to the reader.

Words used at Level 6

next	every
door	don't
very	

NEW WORDS

joke
jewellers
Oscar
sometimes
went
night
dark
closed
mice
too
wind
blew
lightning
flashed
ghosts
made
noise
shapes
tried
frighten
fast
asleep
got
ready
woke
another
TAP
listened
masks
burglars

shall
clock
hide
idea
back
bring
tricks
cried
could
trip
tied
ring
alarm
bell
heard
brave
medal
Saturday
football
match
wave
wish
laughed
cross
happy
sports
full
tennis
roller skate
boxing

golf
snooker
found
whistle
blew
would
real